MW01204623

# God Loves You

# PROMISE JOURNAL

## God Loves You

© 2010 Lake House Gifts
A Division of Ellie Claire™ Gift & Paper Corp.
www.ellieclaire.com

Compiled by Joanie Garborg
Designed by Mick Thurber

All rights reserved. No part of this book may be reproduced in any form without
permission in writing from the publisher.

Scripture references are from the following sources: The Holy Bible, King James Version (KJV). The
Holy Bible, New International Version® NIV®. Copyright © 1973, 1978, 1984 International Bible
Society. Used by permission of Zondervan Bible Publishers. The New American Standard Bible®
(NASB), Copyright © 1960, 1962, 1963, 1968, 1971, 1972, 1973, 1975, 1977, 1995 by The Lockman
Foundation. Used by permission. The Holy Bible, New Living Translation (NLT), copyright 1996, 2004.
Used by permission of Tyndale House Publishers, Inc., Wheaton, Illinois 60189. All rights reserved.
The Message, Copyright © 1993, 1994, 1995, 1996, 2000. 2001, 2002 by Eugene Peterson. Used by
permission of NavPress, Colorado Springs, CO." The New Revised Standard Version Bible: Anglicized
Edition (NRSV), copyright 1989, 1995, Division of Christian Education of the National Council of the
Churches of Christ in the United States of America. Used by permission. The Living Bible (TLB)
© 1971. Used by permission of Tyndale House Publishers, Inc., Wheaton, Illinois.

Excluding Scripture verses, references to men and masculine pronouns have been replaced with gender-
neutral references.

ISBN-13: 978-1-935416-97-5

Printed in China

To

Kathleen

From

Genera with lots of Love

## U N C O N D I T I O N A L   L O V E

God says, "I love you no matter what you do." His love is unconditional and unending.

We are so preciously loved by God that we cannot even comprehend it. No created being can ever know how much and how sweetly and tenderly God loves them. It is only with the help of His grace that we are able to persevere in…endless wonder at the high, surpassing, immeasurable love which our Lord in His goodness has for us.

JULIAN OF NORWICH

The heart of the giver makes the gift dear and precious.

MARTIN LUTHER

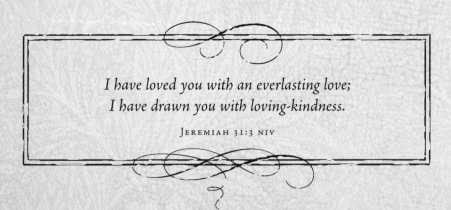

*I have loved you with an everlasting love;*
*I have drawn you with loving-kindness.*

JEREMIAH 31:3 NIV

# UNCONDITIONAL LOVE

_____

_____

_____

_____

_____

_____

_____

_____

_____

_____

_____

_____

_____

_____

_____

_____

_____

_____

_____

_____

## GOD IS FOR YOU

So, what do you think? With God on our side like this, how can
we lose? If God didn't hesitate to put everything on the line for us,
embracing our condition and exposing himself to the worst by sending
his own Son, is there anything else he wouldn't gladly and freely do for
us? And who would dare tangle with God by messing with one of God's
chosen? Who would dare even to point a finger? The One who died for
us—who was raised to life for us!—is in the presence of God at this
very moment sticking up for us.

ROMANS 8:31–34 MSG

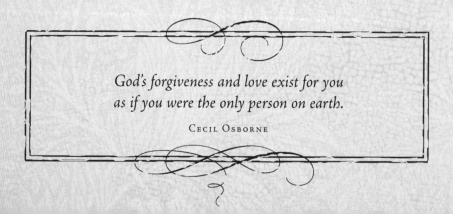

*God's forgiveness and love exist for you*
*as if you were the only person on earth.*

CECIL OSBORNE

GOD IS FOR YOU

_____

_____

_____

_____

_____

_____

_____

_____

_____

_____

_____

_____

_____

_____

_____

_____

_____

_____

_____

## COUNTLESS BEAUTIES

May God give you eyes to see beauty only the heart can understand.

From the world we see, hear, and touch, we behold inspired visions that reveal God's glory. In the sun's light, we catch warm rays of grace and glimpse His eternal design. In the birds' song, we hear His voice and it reawakens our desire for Him. At the wind's touch, we feel His Spirit and sense our eternal existence.

All the world is an utterance of the Almighty. Its countless beauties, its exquisite adaptations, all speak to you of Him.

PHILLIPS BROOKS

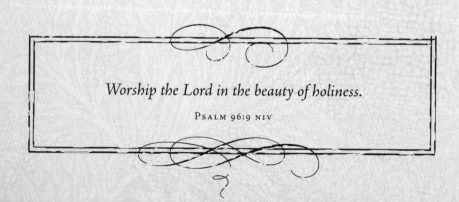

*Worship the Lord in the beauty of holiness.*

PSALM 96:9 NIV

## COUNTLESS BEAUTIES

## THE GRACE OF GOD

But God, being rich in mercy, because of His great love with which He loved us, even when we were dead in our transgressions, made us alive together with Christ (by grace you have been saved), and raised us up with Him, and seated us with Him in the heavenly places in Christ Jesus, so that in the ages to come He might show the surpassing riches of His grace in kindness toward us in Christ Jesus. For by grace you have been saved through faith; and that not of yourselves, it is the gift of God; not as a result of works, so that no one may boast. For we are His workmanship, created in Christ Jesus for good works, which God prepared beforehand so that we would walk in them.

EPHESIANS 2:4–10 NASB

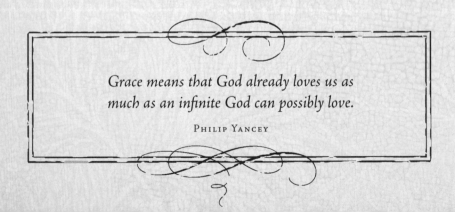

*Grace means that God already loves us as much as an infinite God can possibly love.*

PHILIP YANCEY

# THE GRACE OF GOD

---
---
---
---
---
---
---
---
---
---
---
---
---
---
---
---

## PROMISE OF LOVE

A rainbow stretches from one end of the sky to the other. Each shade of color, each facet of light displays the radiant spectrum of God's love: a promise that He will always love each one of us at our worst and at our best.

Faithful, O Lord, Thy mercies are,

A rock that cannot move!

A thousand promises declare

Thy constancy of love.

CHARLES WESLEY

God's love never ceases. Never.... God doesn't love us less if we fail or more if we succeed. God's love never ceases.

MAX LUCADO

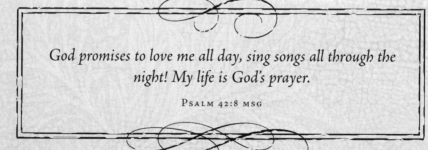

*God promises to love me all day, sing songs all through the night! My life is God's prayer.*

PSALM 42:8 MSG

PROMISE OF LOVE

## TENDER LOVE

For all God's words are right, and everything he does is worthy of our trust. He loves whatever is just and good; the earth is filled with his tender love.

PSALM 33:4–5 TLB

For, lo, the winter is past, the rain is over and gone; the flowers appear on the earth; the time of the singing of birds is come.

SONG OF SOLOMON 2:11–12 KJV

He has remembered his love and his faithfulness…all the ends of the earth have seen the salvation of our God.

PSALM 98:3 NIV

*Love is the sweet, tender, melting nature of God flowing into the creature, making the creature most like unto himself.*

ISAAC PENNINGTON

## TENDER LOVE

The goodness of God is infinitely more wonderful than we will ever be able to comprehend.

A. W. Tozer

All that is good, all that is true, all that is beautiful, all that is beneficent, be it great or small, be it perfect or fragmentary, natural as well as supernatural, moral as well as material, comes from God.

Cardinal John Henry Newman

We walk without fear, full of hope and courage and strength to do His will, waiting for the endless good which He is always giving as fast as He can get us able to take it in.

George MacDonald

*Open your mouth and taste, open your eyes and see—how good God is. Blessed are you who run to him. Worship God if you want the best; worship opens doors to all his goodness.*

Psalm 34:8–9 msg

## THE GOODNESS OF GOD

_____

_____

_____

_____

_____

_____

_____

_____

_____

_____

_____

_____

_____

_____

_____

_____

_____

## THE MAJESTY OF GOD

O Lord, our Lord, how majestic is your name in all the earth! You have set your glory above the heavens…. When I consider your heavens, the work of your fingers, the moon and the stars, which you have set in place, what is man that you are mindful of him, the son of man that you care for him? You made him a little lower than the heavenly beings and crowned him with glory and honor. O Lord, our Lord, how majestic is your name in all the earth!

PSALM 8:1–5, 9 NIV

*Savor little glimpses of God's goodness and His majesty,*
*thankful for the gift of them.*

# THE MAJESTY OF GOD

---

---

---

---

---

---

---

---

---

---

---

---

---

---

---

---

---

---

---

MORNING AND EVENING

We are silent at the beginning of the day because God should have the first word, and we are silent before going to sleep because the last word also belongs to God.... O Lord my God, thank You for bringing this day to a close; thank You for giving me rest in body and soul. Your hand has been over me and has guarded and preserved me.

DIETRICH BONHOEFFER

God loves you in the morning sun and the evening rain, without caution or regret.

BRENNAN MANNING

May none of God's wonderful works keep silence, night or morning. Bright stars, high mountains, the depths of the seas, sources of rushing rivers: May all of these break into song to God, the only Lord of love. And all the angels in the heavens reply: May power, praise, honor, and eternal glory be to God, the only Giver of grace.

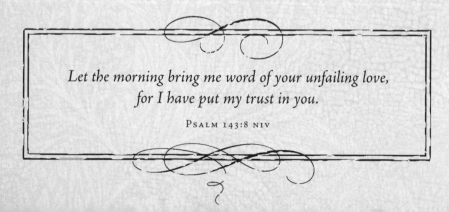

*Let the morning bring me word of your unfailing love,
for I have put my trust in you.*

PSALM 143:8 NIV

# MORNING AND EVENING

_____

_____

_____

_____

_____

_____

_____

_____

_____

_____

_____

_____

_____

_____

_____

_____

_____

_____

_____

_____

_____

## The Faithfulness of God

You, O God, are both tender and kind, not easily angered, immense in love, and you never, never quit.

PSALM 86:15 MSG

It is good to give thanks to the Lord and to sing praises to Your name, O Most High; to declare Your lovingkindness in the morning and Your faithfulness by night.

PSALM 92:1–2 NASB

For the Lord God is a sun and shield; the Lord gives grace and glory; no good thing does He withhold from those who walk uprightly.

PSALM 84:10–11 NASB

The Lord is righteous…He will do no injustice. Every morning He brings His justice to light; He does not fail.

ZEPHANIAH 3:5 NASB

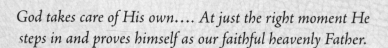

*God takes care of His own…. At just the right moment He steps in and proves himself as our faithful heavenly Father.*

CHARLES R. SWINDOLL

## THE FAITHFULNESS OF GOD

_____

_____

_____

_____

_____

_____

_____

_____

_____

_____

_____

_____

_____

_____

_____

_____

_____

_____

_____

_____

## MADE FOR JOY

Our hearts were made for joy. Our hearts were made to enjoy the One who created them. Too deeply planted to be much affected by the ups and downs of life, this joy is a knowing and a being known by our Creator. He sets our hearts alight with radiant joy.

If one is joyful, it means that one is faithfully living for God, and that nothing else counts; and if one gives joy to others one is doing God's work. With joy without and joy within, all is well.

JANET ERSKINE STUART

Live for today but hold your hands open to tomorrow. Anticipate the future and its changes with joy. There is a seed of God's love in every event, every circumstance, every unpleasant situation in which you may find yourself.

BARBARA JOHNSON

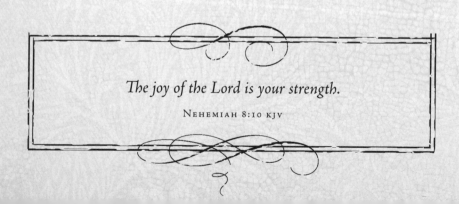

*The joy of the Lord is your strength.*

NEHEMIAH 8:10 KJV

MADE FOR JOY

---

_____

_____

_____

_____

_____

_____

_____

_____

_____

_____

_____

_____

_____

_____

_____

_____

## FRUIT IN SEASON

What happens when we live God's way? He brings gifts into our lives, much the same way that fruit appears in an orchard—things like affection for others, exuberance about life, serenity. We develop a willingness to stick with things, a sense of compassion in the heart, and a conviction that a basic holiness permeates things and people.

GALATIANS 5:22–23 MSG

Oh, the joys of those who do not follow the advice of the wicked, or stand around with sinners, or join in with scoffers. But they delight in doing everything the Lord wants; day and night they think about his law. They are like trees planted along the riverbank, bearing fruit each season without fail. Their leaves never wither, and in all they do, they prosper.

PSALM 1:1–3 NLT

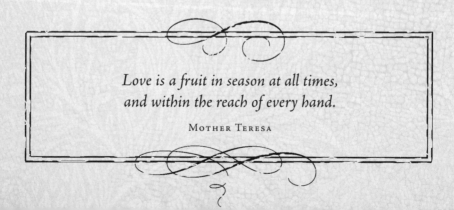

*Love is a fruit in season at all times,*
*and within the reach of every hand.*

MOTHER TERESA

# FRUIT IN SEASON

---

---

---

---

---

---

---

---

---

---

---

---

---

---

---

---

---

---

The mystery of life is that the Lord of life cannot be known except in and through the act of living. Without the concrete and specific involvements of daily life we cannot come to know the loving presence of Him who holds us in the palm of His hand…. Therefore, we are called each day to present to our Lord the whole of our lives.

HENRI J. M. NOUWEN

God promises to keep us in the palm of His hand, with or without our awareness. God has already made a space for us, even if we have not made a space for God.

DAVID AND BARBARA SORENSEN

That Hand which bears all nature up
Shall guard His children well.

WILLIAM COWPER

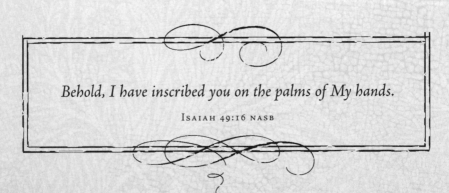

*Behold, I have inscribed you on the palms of My hands.*

ISAIAH 49:16 NASB

## HELD IN HIS HAND

_____

_____

_____

_____

_____

_____

_____

_____

_____

_____

_____

_____

_____

_____

_____

_____

_____

## LOVE ONE ANOTHER

Clothe yourselves with compassion, kindness, humility, gentleness and patience. Bear with each other and forgive whatever grievances you may have against one another. Forgive as the Lord forgave you. And over all these virtues put on love, which binds them all together in perfect unity.

COLOSSIANS 3:12–14 NIV

Love must be sincere…. Honor one another above yourselves.

ROMANS 12:9–10 NIV

May God, who gives this patience and encouragement, help you live in complete harmony with each other.

ROMANS 15:5 NLT

*In God's wisdom, He frequently chooses to meet our needs by showing His love toward us through the hands and hearts of others.*

JACK HAYFORD

LOVE ONE ANOTHER

## A LIFE TRANSFORMED

To pray is to change. This is a great grace. How good of God to provide a path whereby our lives can be taken over by love and joy and peace and patience and kindness and goodness and faithfulness and gentleness and self-control.

RICHARD J. FOSTER

For God is, indeed, a wonderful Father who longs to pour out His mercy upon us, and whose majesty is so great that He can transform us from deep within.

TERESA OF AVILA

A life transformed by the power of God is always a marvel and a miracle.

GERALDINE NICHOLAS

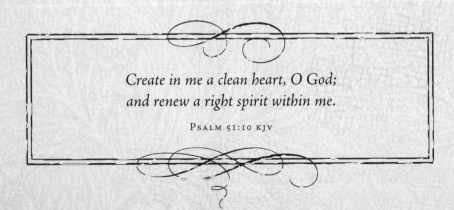

*Create in me a clean heart, O God;*
*and renew a right spirit within me.*

PSALM 51:10 KJV

## A LIFE TRANSFORMED

_____

_____

_____

_____

_____

_____

_____

_____

_____

_____

_____

_____

_____

_____

_____

_____

_____

_____

_____

_____

## GOD'S CARE

The Lord is my shepherd; I shall not want. He maketh me to lie down in green pastures: he leadeth me beside the still waters. He restoreth my soul: he leadeth me in the paths of righteousness for his name's sake. Yea, though I walk through the valley of the shadow of death, I will fear no evil: for thou art with me; thy rod and thy staff they comfort me. Thou preparest a table before me in the presence of mine enemies: thou anointest my head with oil; my cup runneth over. Surely goodness and mercy shall follow me all the days of my life: and I will dwell in the house of the Lord for ever.

PSALM 23:1–6 KJV

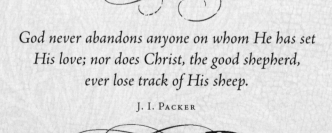

*God never abandons anyone on whom He has set
His love; nor does Christ, the good shepherd,
ever lose track of His sheep.*

J. I. PACKER

# GOD'S CARE

# DIVINE ROMANCE

God's holy beauty comes near you, like a spiritual scent, and it stirs your drowsing soul…. He creates in you the desire to find Him and run after Him—to follow wherever He leads you, and to press peacefully against His heart wherever He is. If you are seeking after God, you may be sure of this: God is seeking you much more. He is the Lover, and you are His beloved. He has promised himself to you.

JOHN OF THE CROSS

To fall in love with God is the greatest of all romances—to seek Him the greatest of all adventures, to find Him the greatest human achievement.

AUGUSTINE

In the morning let our hearts gaze upon God's love…and in the beauty of that vision, let us go forth to meet the day.

ROY LESSIN

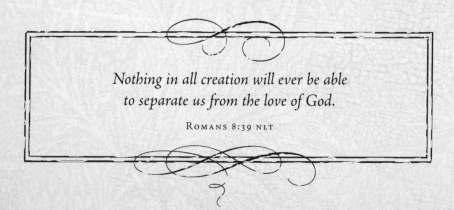

*Nothing in all creation will ever be able to separate us from the love of God.*

ROMANS 8:39 NLT

## DIVINE ROMANCE

_____

_____

_____

_____

_____

_____

_____

_____

_____

_____

_____

_____

_____

_____

_____

_____

## GOD SO LOVED

For God so loved the world, that he gave his only begotten Son, that whosoever believeth in him should not perish, but have everlasting life.  For God sent not his Son into the world to condemn the world; but that the world through him might be saved.

JOHN 3:16–17 KJV

This is My commandment, that you love one another, just as I have loved you. Greater love has no one than this, that one lay down his life for his friends.

JOHN 15:12–13 NASB

May the Lord direct your hearts into the love of God.

2 THESSALONIANS 3:5 NASB

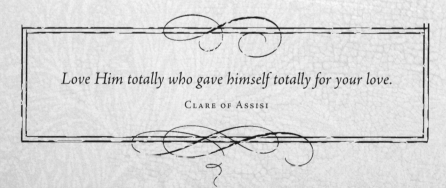

*Love Him totally who gave himself totally for your love.*

CLARE OF ASSISI

GOD SO LOVED

_____

_____

_____

_____

_____

_____

_____

_____

_____

_____

_____

_____

_____

_____

_____

_____

God, who has led you safely on so far, will lead you on to the end. Be altogether at rest in the loving holy confidence which you ought to have in His heavenly Providence.

FRANCIS DE SALES

Guidance is a sovereign act. Not merely does God will to guide us by showing us His way…whatever mistakes we may make, we shall come safely home. Slippings and strayings there will be, no doubt, but the everlasting arms are beneath us; we shall be caught, rescued, restored. This is God's promise; this is how good He is. And our self-distrust, while keeping us humble, must not cloud the joy with which we lean on our faithful covenant God.

J. I. PACKER

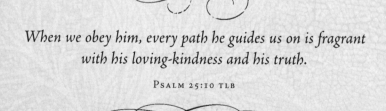

*When we obey him, every path he guides us on is fragrant with his loving-kindness and his truth.*

PSALM 25:10 TLB

# FAITHFUL GUIDE

## RESTORATION

The Spirit of the Sovereign Lord is on me, because the Lord has anointed me to preach good news to the poor. He has sent me to bind up the brokenhearted, to proclaim freedom for the captives and release from darkness for the prisoners, to proclaim the year of the Lord's favor and the day of vengeance of our God, to comfort all who mourn, and provide for those who grieve in Zion—to bestow on them a crown of beauty instead of ashes, the oil of gladness instead of mourning, and a garment of praise instead of a spirit of despair. They will be called oaks of righteousness, a planting of the Lord for the display of his splendor.

ISAIAH 61:1–3 NIV

*The Lord promises to bind up the brokenhearted, to give relief and full deliverance to those whose spirits have been weighed down.*

CHARLES R. SWINDOLL

# RESTORATION

As the beloved of God, under the shadow of His wings—

As a well-watered garden,

and as the apple of God's eye—

the seeds of great faith live within us.

You are a child of your heavenly Father. Confide in Him. Your faith in His
love and power can never be bold enough.

BASILEA SCHLINK

The well of Providence is deep. It's the buckets we bring to it that are small.

MARY WEBB

*It's impossible to please God apart from faith…. Anyone
who wants to approach God must believe both that he exists
and that he cares enough to respond to those who seek him.*

HEBREWS 11:6 MSG

# SEEDS OF FAITH

## SEEK AND FIND

All things you ask in prayer, believing, you will receive.

MATTHEW 21:22 NASB

Ask, and it will be given to you; seek, and you will find; knock, and it will be opened to you. For everyone who asks, receives; and he who seeks, finds; and to him who knocks, it will be opened.

LUKE 11:9–10 KJV

And ye shall seek me, and find me, when ye shall search for me with all your heart. And I will be found of you, saith the Lord.

JEREMIAH 29:13 KJV

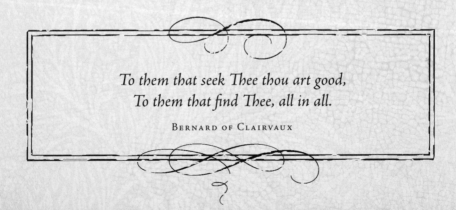

*To them that seek Thee thou art good,*
*To them that find Thee, all in all.*

BERNARD OF CLAIRVAUX

# SEEK AND FIND

_____

_____

_____

_____

_____

_____

_____

_____

_____

_____

_____

_____

_____

_____

_____

_____

_____

_____

## ENFOLDED IN PEACE

I will let God's peace infuse every part of today. As the chaos swirls and life's demands pull at me on all sides, I will breathe in God's peace that surpasses all understanding. He has promised that He would set within me a peace too deeply planted to be affected by unexpected or exhausting demands.

Calm me, O Lord, as you stilled the storm,
Still me, O Lord, keep me from harm.
Let all the tumult within me cease,
Enfold me, Lord, in your peace.

CELTIC TRADITIONAL

God cannot give us a happiness and peace apart from himself, because it is not there. There is no such thing.

C. S. LEWIS

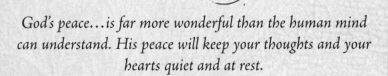

*God's peace…is far more wonderful than the human mind can understand. His peace will keep your thoughts and your hearts quiet and at rest.*

PHILIPPIANS 4:7 TLB

# ENFOLDED IN PEACE

## SEEK FIRST

Look at the birds of the air, that they do not sow, nor reap nor gather into barns, and yet your heavenly Father feeds them. Are you not worth much more than they? And who of you by being worried can add a single hour to his life? And why are you worried about clothing? Observe how the lilies of the field grow; they do not toil nor do they spin, yet I say to you that not even Solomon in all his glory clothed himself like one of these. But if God so clothes the grass of the field, which is alive today and tomorrow is thrown into the furnace, will He not much more clothe you? You of little faith! Do not worry then, saying, "What will we eat?" or "What will we drink?" or "What will we wear for clothing?" For…your heavenly Father knows that you need all these things. But seek first His kingdom and His righteousness, and all these things will be added to you.

MATTHEW 6:26–33 NASB

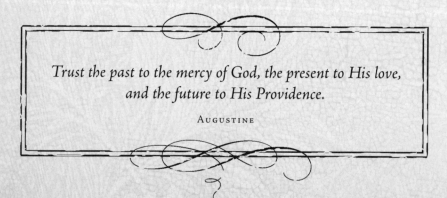

*Trust the past to the mercy of God, the present to His love, and the future to His Providence.*

AUGUSTINE

SEEK FIRST

Friendship with God is a two-way street.... Jesus said that He tells His friends all that His Father has told Him; close friends communicate thoroughly and make a transfer of heart and thought. How awesome is our opportunity to be friends with God, the almighty Creator of all!

BEVERLY LaHAYE

We can look to God as our Father. We can have a personal sense of His love for us and His interest in us, for He is concerned about us as a father is concerned for his children.... Incredible as it may seem, God wants our companionship. He wants to have us close to Him. He wants to be a father to us, to shield us, to protect us, to counsel us, and to guide us in our way through life.

BILLY GRAHAM

God's friendship is the unexpected joy we find when we reach His outstretched hand.

JANET L. WEAVER SMITH

*I have called you friends, for all things that I have heard from My Father I have made known to you.*

JOHN 15:15 NASB

## FRIENDSHIP WITH GOD

_____

_____

_____

_____

_____

_____

_____

_____

_____

_____

_____

_____

_____

_____

_____

_____

_____

_____

_____

_____

_____

_____

_____

# THE LOVE OF GOD

God's love is meteoric,

his loyalty astronomic,

His purpose titanic,

his verdicts oceanic.

Yet in his largeness

nothing gets lost.

PSALM 36:5–6 MSG

May your roots go down deep into the soil of God's marvelous love. And

may you have the power to understand, as all God's people should, how

wide, how long, how high, and how deep his love really is.

EPHESIANS 3:17–18 NLT

*The love of God is broader than the measure of our mind*
*And the heart of the Eternal is most wonderfully kind.*

FREDERICK W. FABER

# THE LOVE OF GOD

_____

_____

_____

_____

_____

_____

_____

_____

_____

_____

_____

_____

_____

_____

_____

_____

_____

## WONDER AND PRAISE

If you have never heard the mountains singing, or seen the trees of the field clapping their hands, do not think because of that they don't. Ask God to open your ears so you may hear it, and your eyes so you may see it, because, though few people ever know it, they do, my friend, they do.

PHILLIPS MCCANDLISH

The love of the Father is like a sudden rain shower that will pour forth when you least expect it, catching you up into wonder and praise.

RICHARD J. FOSTER

The wonder of living is held within the beauty of silence, the glory of sunlight…the sweetness of fresh spring air, the quiet strength of earth, and the love that lies at the very root of all things.

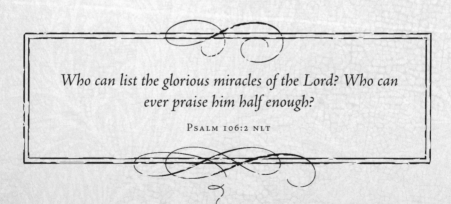

*Who can list the glorious miracles of the Lord? Who can ever praise him half enough?*

PSALM 106:2 NLT

## WONDER AND PRAISE

_____

_____

_____

_____

_____

_____

_____

_____

_____

_____

_____

_____

_____

_____

_____

_____

## PROTECTION

The Lord is my light and my salvation—whom shall I fear? The Lord is the stronghold of my life—of whom shall I be afraid? One thing I ask of the Lord, this is what I seek: that I may dwell in the house of the Lord all the days of my life, to gaze upon the beauty of the Lord and to seek him in his temple. For in the day of trouble he will keep me safe in his dwelling; he will hide me in the shelter of his tabernacle and set me high upon a rock. Hear my voice when I call, O Lord; be merciful to me and answer me. My heart says of you, "Seek his face!" Your face, Lord, I will seek.

PSALM 27:1, 4–5, 7–8 NIV

*Leave behind your fear and dwell on the lovingkindness of God, that you may recover by gazing on Him.*

# PROTECTION

---

---

---

---

---

---

---

---

---

---

---

---

---

---

---

---

---

---

The light of God surrounds me,

The love of God enfolds me,

The presence of God watches over me,

Wherever I am, God is.

He is everything that is good and comfortable for us. He is our clothing

that for love wraps us, clasps us, and all surrounds us for tender love.

JULIAN OF NORWICH

The Lord's goodness surrounds us at every moment. I walk through it

almost with difficulty, as through thick grass and flowers.

R. W. BARBER

What can harm us when everything must first touch God whose presence

surrounds us?

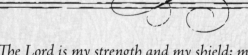

*The Lord is my strength and my shield; my heart trusted in*
*him, and I am helped.*

PSALM 28:7 KJV

SURROUNDED BY LOVE

_____

_____

_____

_____

_____

_____

_____

_____

_____

_____

_____

_____

_____

_____

_____

_____

_____

_____

_____

_____

God's love, though, is ever and always, eternally present to all who fear him, making everything right for them and their children as they follow his Covenant ways and remember to do whatever he said.

PSALM 103:17–18 MSG

If you are pleased with me, teach me your ways so I may know you and continue to find favor with you.

EXODUS 33:13 NIV

Yes, Lord, walking in the way of your laws, we wait for you; your name and renown are the desire of our hearts.

ISAIAH 26:8 NIV

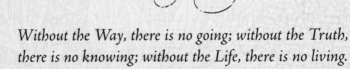

*Without the Way, there is no going; without the Truth, there is no knowing; without the Life, there is no living.*

THOMAS À KEMPIS

WALKING IN HIS WAYS

## INVALUABLE LOVE

God loves us for ourselves. He values our love more than He values galaxies of new created worlds.

A. W. TOZER

If you believe in God, it is not too difficult to believe that He is concerned about the universe and all the events on this earth. But the really staggering message of the Bible is that this same God cares deeply about you and your identity and the events of your life…. We have missed the full impact of the Gospel if we have not discovered what it is to be ourselves, loved by God, irreplaceable in His sight, unique among our fellowmen.

BRUCE LARSON

Our greatness rests solely on the fact that God in His incomprehensible goodness has bestowed His love upon us. God does not love us because we are so valuable; we are valuable because God loves us.

HELMUT THIELICKE

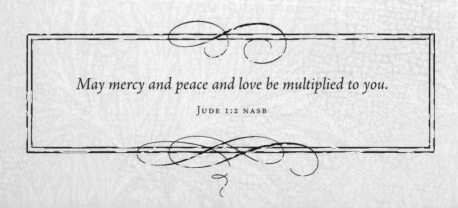

*May mercy and peace and love be multiplied to you.*

JUDE 1:2 NASB

INVALUABLE LOVE

## My Help

I will lift up mine eyes unto the hills, from whence cometh my help. My

help cometh from the Lord, which made heaven and earth. He will not

suffer thy foot to be moved: he that keepeth thee will not slumber. Behold,

he that keepeth Israel shall neither slumber nor sleep. The Lord is thy

keeper: the Lord is thy shade upon thy right hand. The sun shall not smite

thee by day, nor the moon by night. The Lord shall preserve thee from all

evil: he shall preserve thy soul. The Lord shall preserve thy going out and

thy coming in from this time forth, and even for evermore.

Psalm 121:1–8 kjv

*We have a Father in heaven who is almighty,*
*who loves His children as He loves His only-begotten Son,*
*and whose very joy and delight it is to…help them at all*
*times and under all circumstances.*

George Müeller

# MY HELP

_____

_____

_____

_____

_____

_____

_____

_____

_____

_____

_____

_____

_____

_____

_____

_____

_____

Solitude liberates us from entanglements by carving out a space from which we can see ourselves and our situation before the Audience of One. Solitude provides the private place where we can take our bearings and so make God our North Star.

OS GUINNESS

Settle yourself in solitude and you will come upon Him in yourself.

TERESA OF AVILA

We must drink deeply from the very Source the deep calm and peace of interior quietude and refreshment of God, allowing the pure water of divine grace to flow plentifully and unceasingly from the Source itself.

MOTHER TERESA

*Whoever drinks of the water that I will give him shall never thirst; but the water that I will give him will become in him a well of water springing up to eternal life.*

JOHN 4:13–14 NASB

SETTLED IN SOLITUDE

_____

_____

_____

_____

_____

_____

_____

_____

_____

_____

_____

_____

_____

_____

_____

_____

_____

_____

_____

## RESTORATION

God made my life complete when

I placed all the pieces before him.

God rewrote the text of my life

when I opened the book of my heart to his eyes.

PSALM 18:20, 24 MSG

Now the God of peace…make you perfect in every good work to do his

will, working in you that which is wellpleasing in his sight, through Jesus

Christ; to whom be glory for ever and ever. Amen.

HEBREWS 13:20–21 KJV

*God puts each fresh morning, each new chance of life, into*
*our hands as a gift.*

## RESTORATION

_____

_____

_____

_____

_____

_____

_____

_____

_____

_____

_____

_____

_____

_____

_____

_____

_____

_____

There is nothing but God's grace. We walk upon it; we breathe it; we live and die by it; it makes the nails and axles of the universe.

ROBERT LOUIS STEVENSON

Grace is no stationary thing, it is ever becoming. It is flowing straight out of God's heart. Grace does nothing but re-form and convey God. Grace makes the soul conformable to the will of God. God, the ground of the soul, and grace go together.

MEISTER ECKHART

Grace and gratitude belong together like heaven and earth. Grace evokes gratitude like the voice an echo. Gratitude follows grace as thunder follows lightning.

KARL BARTH

*God is sheer mercy and grace; not easily angered, he's rich in love.... As far as sunrise is from sunset, he has separated us from our sins.*

PSALM 103:8, 12 MSG

# NOTHING BUT GRACE

## SHOWERS OF BLESSINGS

Bless the Lord, O my soul: and all that is within me, bless his holy name. Bless the Lord, O my soul, and forget not all his benefits: Who forgiveth all thine iniquities; who healeth all thy diseases; who redeemeth thy life from destruction; who crowneth thee with lovingkindness and tender mercies; who satisfieth thy mouth with good things; so that thy youth is renewed like the eagle's.

PSALM 103:1–5 KJV

I will send showers, showers of blessings, which will come just when they are needed.

EZEKIEL 34:26 NLT

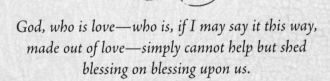

*God, who is love—who is, if I may say it this way,*
*made out of love—simply cannot help but shed*
*blessing on blessing upon us.*

HANNAH WHITALL SMITH

SHOWERS OF BLESSINGS

## SEE HOW HE LOVES US!

Blue skies with white clouds on summer days. A myriad of stars on clear
moonlit nights. Tulips and roses and violets and dandelions and daisies.
Bluebirds and laughter and sunshine and Easter. See how He loves us!

ALICE CHAPIN

His tenderness in the springing grass,

His beauty in the flowers,

His living love in the sun above—

All here, and near, and ours.

CHARLOTTE PERKINS GILMAN

O God, creator of light: at the rising of Your sun this morning, let the
greatest of all lights, Your love, rise like the sun within our hearts.

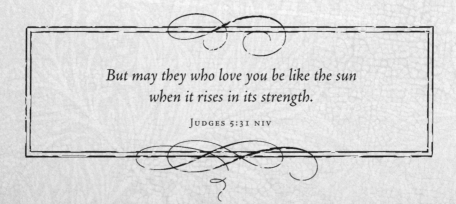

*But may they who love you be like the sun
when it rises in its strength.*

JUDGES 5:31 NIV

SEE HOW HE LOVES US!

---
---
---

---
---

---
---

---
---

---
---

---
---

---
---

---
---

---
---

---
---

---
---

## The Right Word

Like apples of gold in settings of silver is a word spoken in right circumstances. Like an earring of gold and an ornament of fine gold is a wise reprover to a listening ear. Like the cold of snow in the time of harvest is a faithful messenger to those who send him.

PROVERBS 25:11–13 NASB

Let everything you say be good and helpful, so that your words will be an encouragement to those who hear them.

EPHESIANS 4:29 NLT

Whatever you do, whether in word or deed, do it all in the name of the Lord Jesus, giving thanks to God the Father through him.

COLOSSIANS 3:17 NIV

*Walk softly. Speak tenderly. Love fervently.*

All enjoyment spontaneously overflows into praise…. The world rings with praise…walkers praising the countryside, players praising their favorite game…. I think we delight to praise what we enjoy because the praise not merely expresses but completes the enjoyment; it is the appointed consummation.

C. S. LEWIS

God's pursuit of praise from us and our pursuit of pleasure in Him are one and the same pursuit. God's quest to be glorified and our quest to be satisfied reach their goal in this one experience: our delight in God which overflows in praise.

JOHN PIPER

Earth, with her thousand voices, praises God.

SAMUEL TAYLOR COLERIDGE

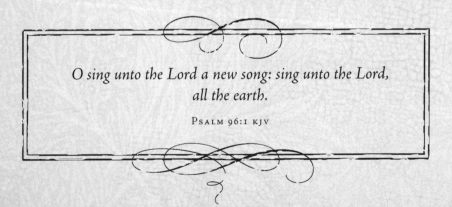

*O sing unto the Lord a new song: sing unto the Lord, all the earth.*

PSALM 96:1 KJV

OVERFLOWING PRAISE

## LOVE NEVER FAILS

If I speak with the tongues of men and of angels, but do not have love,
I have become a noisy gong or a clanging cymbal. If I have the gift of
prophecy, and know all mysteries and all knowledge; and if I have all faith,
so as to remove mountains, but do not have love, I am nothing. And if I
give all my possessions to feed the poor, and if I surrender my body to be
burned, but do not have love, it profits me nothing. Love is patient, love is
kind and is not jealous; love does not brag and is not arrogant, does not act
unbecomingly; it does not seek its own, is not provoked, does not take into
account a wrong suffered, does not rejoice in unrighteousness, but rejoices
with the truth; bears all things, believes all things, hopes all things, endures
all things. Love never fails.

1 CORINTHIANS 13:1–8 NASB

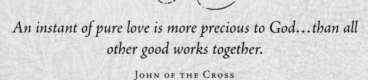

*An instant of pure love is more precious to God…than all
other good works together.*

JOHN OF THE CROSS

LOVE NEVER FAILS

_____

_____

_____

_____

_____

_____

_____

_____

_____

_____

_____

_____

_____

_____

_____

_____

_____

_____

# The Garden of His Love

May you be ever present in the garden of His love.

It is God's knowledge of me, His careful husbanding of the ground of my being,

His constant presence in the garden of my little life that guarantees my joy.

W. Phillip Keller

It's only a tiny rosebud—

A flower of God's design;

But I cannot unfold the petals

With these clumsy hands of mine.

And the pathway that lies before me

Only my Heavenly Father knows—

I'll trust Him to unfold the moments

Just as He unfolds the rose.

*The Lord will guide you always; he will satisfy your needs
in a sun-scorched land.... You will be like a well-watered
garden, like a spring whose waters never fail.*

Isaiah 58:11 niv

THE GARDEN OF HIS LOVE

---

---

---

---

---

---

---

---

---

---

---

---

---

---

---

---

---

---

---

---

## GOD IS OUR REFUGE

Hear my cry, O God; Give heed to my prayer. From the end of the earth I call to You when my heart is faint; lead me to the rock that is higher than I. For You have been a refuge for me, a tower of strength against the enemy. Let me dwell in Your tent forever; let me take refuge in the shelter of Your wings.

PSALM 61:1–4 NASB

Whom have I in heaven but You? And besides You, I desire nothing on earth. My flesh and my heart may fail, but God is the strength of my heart and my portion forever. As for me, the nearness of God is my good; I have made the Lord God my refuge.

PSALM 73:25–26, 28 NASB

*When God has become…our refuge and our fortress, then we can reach out to Him in the midst of a broken world and feel at home while still on the way.*

HENRI J. M. NOUWEN

GOD IS OUR REFUGE

## SOUGHT AND FOUND

It is God's will that we believe that we see Him continually, though it seems to us that the sight be only partial; and through this belief He makes us always to gain more grace, for God wishes to be seen, and He wishes to be sought, and He wishes to be expected, and He wishes to be trusted.

JULIAN OF NORWICH

To seek God means first of all to let yourself be found by Him.

God's nature is given me. His love is jealous for my life. All His attributes are woven into the pattern of my spirit. What a God is this! His life implanted in every child. Thank you, Father, for this.

JIM ELLIOT

*Seek the Lord your God, and you will find Him if you seek Him with all your heart and with all your soul.*

DEUTERONOMY 4:29 NIV

# SOUGHT AND FOUND

_____

_____

_____

_____

_____

_____

_____

_____

_____

_____

_____

_____

_____

_____

_____

_____

_____

_____

_____

_____

_____

_____

## FREE TO LIVE

God, your God, will cut away the thick calluses on your heart and your children's hearts, freeing you to love God, your God, with your whole heart and soul and live, really live…. And you will make a new start, listening obediently to God, keeping all his commandments that I'm commanding you today. God, your God, will outdo himself in making things go well for you…. Love God, your God. Walk in his ways. Keep his commandments, regulations, and rules so that you will live, really live, live exuberantly, blessed by God …. Love God, your God, listening obediently to him, firmly embracing him. Oh yes, he is life itself.

DEUTERONOMY 30:6–9, 16, 20 MSG

*I asked God for all things that I might enjoy life. He gave me life that I might enjoy all things.*

# FREE TO LIVE

## SHEPHERD OF LOVE

The King of love my Shepherd is,

Whose goodness faileth never;

I nothing lack if I am His,

And He is mine forever.

HENRY WILLIAMS BAKER

Abandon yourself to His care and guidance, as a sheep in the care of a

shepherd, and trust Him utterly.

HANNAH WHITALL SMITH

God is the shepherd in search of His lamb. His legs are scratched, His feet

are sore and His eyes are burning. He scales the cliffs and traverses the

fields. He explores the caves. He cups His hands to His mouth and calls

into the canyon. And the name He calls is yours.

MAX LUCADO

*He calls his own sheep by name and leads them out.... His*
*sheep follow him because they know his voice.*

JOHN 10:3–4 NIV

SHEPHERD OF LOVE

## New Creation

For Christ's love compels us, because we are convinced that one died for all, and therefore all died. And he died for all, that those who live should no longer live for themselves but for him who died for them and was raised again. Therefore, if anyone is in Christ, he is a new creation.

2 Corinthians 5:14–15, 17 niv

Forget the former things; do not dwell on the past. See, I am doing a new thing!

Isaiah 43:18 niv

*Always new. Always exciting. Always full of promise. The mornings of our lives, each a personal daily miracle!*

Gloria Gaither

## NEW CREATION

---
---
---
---
---
---
---
---
---
---
---
---
---
---
---
---
---
---
---
---
---
---
---

## The Beauty of God's Peace

In comparison with this big world, the human heart is only a small thing. Though the world is so large, it is utterly unable to satisfy this tiny heart. Our ever growing soul and its capacities can be satisfied only in the infinite God. As water is restless until it reaches its level, so the soul has no peace until it rests in God.

Sadhu Sundar Singh

Peace is a margin of power around our daily need. Peace is a consciousness of springs too deep for earthly droughts to dry up.

Harry Emerson Fosdick

Drop Thy still dews of quietness

till all our strivings cease;

take from our souls the strain and stress,

and let our ordered lives confess

the beauty of Thy peace.

John Greenleaf Whittier

*Be still, and know that I am God.*

Psalm 46:10 KJV

# THE BEAUTY OF GOD'S PEACE

## A RIVER OF DELIGHTS

Your love, O Lord, reaches to the heavens, your faithfulness to the skies.

Your righteousness is like the mighty mountains, your justice like the great

deep…. How priceless is your unfailing love! Both high and low among

men find refuge in the shadow of your wings. They feast on the abundance

of your house; you give them drink from your river of delights. For with

you is the fountain of life; in your light we see light.

PSALM 36:5–9 NIV

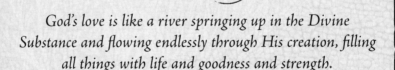

*God's love is like a river springing up in the Divine*
*Substance and flowing endlessly through His creation, filling*
*all things with life and goodness and strength.*

THOMAS MERTON

# A River of Delights

## A QUIET SANCTUARY

Deep within us all there is an amazing inner sanctuary of the soul, a holy place...to which we may continuously return. Eternity is at our hearts, pressing upon our time-torn lives, warming us...calling us home unto Itself. Yielding to these persuasions...utterly and completely, to the Light within, is the beginning of true life.... Life from the Center is a life of unhurried peace, and power. It is simple. It is serene.... We need not get frantic. He is at the helm. And when our little day is done we lie down quietly in peace, for all is well.

THOMAS R. KELLY

Don't get so busy that you miss the beauty of a day or the serenity of a quiet moment alone. For it is often life's smallest pleasures and gentlest joys that make the biggest and most lasting difference.

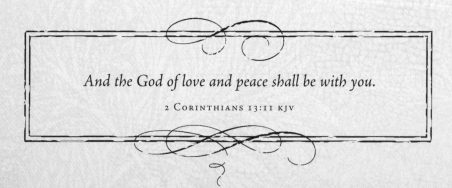

*And the God of love and peace shall be with you.*

2 CORINTHIANS 13:11 KJV

# A QUIET SANCTUARY

## FAITHFULNESS

I will sing of the mercies of the Lord for ever: with my mouth will I make known thy faithfulness to all generations.

Psalm 89:1 KJV

Not to us, O Lord, not to us, but to Your name give glory because of Your lovingkindness, because of Your truth.

Psalm 115:1 NASB

For your unfailing love is as high as the heavens. Your faithfulness reaches to the clouds. Be exalted, O God, above the highest heavens. May your glory shine over all the earth.

Psalm 57:10–11 NLT

*Be assured, if you walk with Him and look to Him and expect help from Him, He will never fail you.*

George Müeller

# FAITHFULNESS

---

---

---

---

---

---

---

---

---

---

---

---

---

---

---

---

---

---

---

---

---

---

---

---

---

Morning has broken like the first morning,
Blackbird has spoken like the first bird....
Praise with elation, praise every morning,
God's re-creation of the new day!

ELEANOR FARJEON

Always new. Always exciting. Always full of promise. The mornings of our lives, each a personal daily miracle!

GLORIA GAITHER

That is God's call to us—simply to be people who are content to live close to Him and to renew the kind of life in which the closeness is felt and experienced.

THOMAS MERTON

*The steadfast love of the Lord never ceases,*
*his mercies never come to an end; they are*
*new every morning; great is your faithfulness.*

LAMENTATIONS 3:22–23 NRSV

N E W   E V E R Y   M O R N I N G

## THE LORD'S PRAYER

Our Father which art in heaven, Hallowed be thy name. Thy kingdom come. Thy will be done in earth, as it is in heaven. Give us this day our daily bread. And forgive us our debts, as we forgive our debtors. And lead us not into temptation, but deliver us from evil: For thine is the kingdom, and the power, and the glory, for ever. Amen.

MATTHEW 6:9–13 KJV

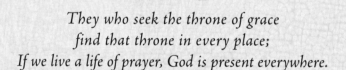

*They who seek the throne of grace*
*find that throne in every place;*
*If we live a life of prayer, God is present everywhere.*

OLIVER HOLDEN

# THE LORD'S PRAYER

Thank you, God, for little things
That often come our way,
The things we take for granted
But don't mention when we pray.

The unexpected courtesy,
The thoughtful kindly deed,
A hand reached out to help us
In the time of sudden need.

Oh, make us more aware, dear God,
Of little daily graces
That come to us with sweet surprise
From never-dreamed-of places.

Gratitude…takes nothing for granted, is never unresponsive, is constantly awakening to new wonder and to praise of the goodness of God.

THOMAS MERTON

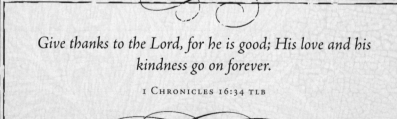

*Give thanks to the Lord, for he is good; His love and his kindness go on forever.*

1 CHRONICLES 16:34 TLB

GRATITUDE FOR DAILY GRACES

_____

_____

_____

_____

_____

_____

_____

_____

_____

_____

_____

_____

_____

_____

_____

_____

_____

_____

# KNOW THE LORD

I will betroth you to Me forever; yes, I will betroth you to Me in righteousness and in justice, in lovingkindness and in compassion, and I will betroth you to Me in faithfulness. Then you will know the Lord.

HOSEA 2:19–20 NASB

Let him that glorieth glory in this, that he understandeth and knoweth me, that I am the Lord which exercise lovingkindness, judgment, and righteousness, in the earth: for in these things I delight.

JEREMIAH 9:23–24 KJV

So let us know, let us press on to know the Lord. His going forth is as certain as the dawn; and He will come to us like the rain, like the spring rain watering the earth.

HOSEA 6:3 NASB

*In our unquenchable longing to know God personally, we pursue Him with passion and find He is relentless in His pursuit of us.*

# KNOW THE LORD

## LOVE WITHOUT LIMITS

Before anything else, above all else, beyond everything else, God loves us. God loves us extravagantly, ridiculously, without limit or condition. God is in love with us…God yearns for us.

ROBERTA BONDI

There is no limit to God's love. It is without measure and its depth cannot be sounded.

MOTHER TERESA

Everything which relates to God is infinite. We must therefore, while we keep our hearts humble, keep our aims high. Our highest services are indeed but finite, imperfect. But as God is unlimited in goodness, He should have our unlimited love.

HANNAH MORE

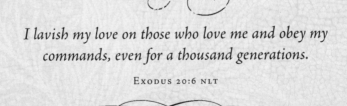

*I lavish my love on those who love me and obey my commands, even for a thousand generations.*

EXODUS 20:6 NLT

LOVE WITHOUT LIMITS

_____
_____
_____
_____
_____
_____
_____
_____
_____
_____
_____
_____
_____
_____
_____
_____
_____
_____
_____
_____
_____

The God who made the world and everything in it is the Lord of heaven and earth.... He himself gives all men life and breath and everything else.... God did this so that men would seek him and perhaps reach out for him and find him, though he is not far from each one of us. "For in him we live, and move, and have our being."

ACTS 17:24–28 NIV

I love those who love me; and those who diligently seek me will find me.

PROVERBS 8:17 NASB

*God is not an elusive dream or a phantom to chase, but a divine person to know. He does not avoid us, but seeks us. When we seek Him, the contact is instantaneous.*

NEVA COYLE

SEEK THE LORD

## GOD IS ENOUGH

He who has God and everything has no more than he who has God alone.

C. S. LEWIS

God, of Your goodness give me Yourself, for You are enough for me. And only in You do I have everything.

JULIAN OF NORWICH

To know Him is to love Him and to know Him better

is to love Him more. We can get a right start only by

accepting God as He is and learning to love Him for

what He is. As we go on to know Him better we shall

find it a source of unspeakable joy that God is just what

He is…. O God, I have tasted Thy goodness, and it has

both satisfied me and made me thirsty for more.

A.W. TOZER

*As the deer pants for streams of water, so my soul pants for*
*you, O God. My soul thirsts for God, for the living God.*

PSALM 42:1–2 NIV

GOD IS ENOUGH

## LIVE IN HARMONY

The wisdom that comes from heaven is first of all pure. It is also peace loving, gentle at all times, and willing to yield to others. It is full of mercy and good deeds. It shows no partiality and is always sincere.

JAMES 3:17 NLT

Finally, all of you, live in harmony with one another; be sympathetic, love... be compassionate and humble. Do not repay evil with evil or insult with insult, but with blessing, because to this you were called so that you may inherit a blessing.

1 PETER 3:8–9 NIV

*To love other people means to see*
*them as God intended them to be.*

LIVE IN HARMONY

## GOD LISTENS

Open wide the windows of our spirits and fill us full of light; open wide the door of our hearts, that we may receive and entertain Thee with all our powers of adoration.

CHRISTINA ROSSETTI

We come this morning—
Like empty pitchers to a full fountain,
With no merits of our own,
O Lord—open up a window of heaven…
And listen this morning.

JAMES WELDON JOHNSON

God listens in compassion and love, just like we do when our children come to us. He delights in our presence.

RICHARD J. FOSTER

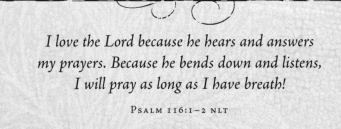

*I love the Lord because he hears and answers
my prayers. Because he bends down and listens,
I will pray as long as I have breath!*

PSALM 116:1–2 NLT

GOD LISTENS

## DELIGHT IN THE LORD

Delight yourself in the Lord and he will give you the desires of your heart. Commit your way to the Lord; trust in him and he will do this: He will make your righteousness shine like the dawn, the justice of your cause like the noonday sun.

PSALM 37:4–6 NIV

Send forth your light and your truth, let them guide me; let them bring me to your holy mountain, to the place where you dwell. Then will I go to the altar of God, to God, my joy and my delight.

PSALM 43:3–4 NIV

*Our fulfillment comes in knowing God's glory, loving Him for it, and delighting in it.*

DELIGHT IN THE LORD

_____

_____

_____

_____

_____

_____

_____

_____

_____

_____

_____

_____

_____

_____

_____

_____

_____

_____

# By Love Alone

By love alone is God enjoyed; by love alone delighted in, by love alone approached and admired. His nature requires love.

THOMAS TRAHERNE

Love does not allow lovers
to belong anymore to themselves,
but they belong only to the Beloved.

DIONYSIUS

There is an essential connection between experiencing God, loving God, and trusting God. You will trust God only as much as you love Him, and you will love Him to the extent you have touched Him, rather than He has touched you.

BRENNAN MANNING

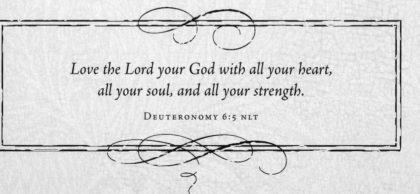

*Love the Lord your God with all your heart,
all your soul, and all your strength.*

DEUTERONOMY 6:5 NLT

BY LOVE ALONE

Be strong and courageous! Do not tremble or be dismayed, for the Lord your God is with you wherever you go.

JOSHUA 1:9 NASB

The Lord your God is with you, he is mighty to save. He will take great delight in you, he will quiet you with his love, he will rejoice over you with singing.

ZEPHANIAH 3:17 NIV

How we thank you, Lord! Your mighty miracles give proof that you care.

PSALM 75:1 TLB

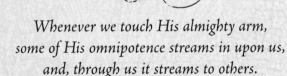

*Whenever we touch His almighty arm,*
*some of His omnipotence streams in upon us,*
*and, through us it streams to others.*

OLE HALLESBY

MIGHTY TO SAVE

## TOTALLY AWARE

God is every moment totally aware of each one of us. Totally aware in intense concentration and love…. No one passes through any area of life, happy or tragic, without the attention of God with him.

EUGENIA PRICE

Because God is responsible for our welfare, we are told to cast all our care upon Him, for He cares for us. God says, "I'll take the burden—don't give it a thought—leave it to Me." God is keenly aware that we are dependent upon Him for life's necessities.

BILLY GRAHAM

You are God's created beauty and the focus of His affection and delight.

JANET L. WEAVER SMITH

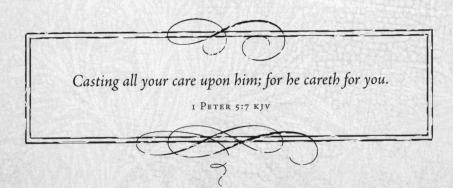

*Casting all your care upon him; for he careth for you.*

1 PETER 5:7 KJV

# TOTALLY AWARE

## THE LOVE OF GOD

Who shall separate us from the love of Christ? Shall trouble or hardship or persecution or famine or nakedness or danger or sword? No, in all these things we are more than conquerors through him who loved us. For I am convinced that neither death nor life, neither angels nor demons, neither the present nor the future, nor any powers, neither height nor depth, nor anything else in all creation, will be able to separate us from the love of God that is in Christ Jesus our Lord.

ROMANS 8:35, 37–39 NIV

*Nothing can separate you from His love, absolutely nothing.... God is enough for time, and God is enough for eternity. God is enough!*

HANNAH WHITALL SMITH

THE LOVE OF GOD

## TREASURE IN NATURE

If we are children of God, we have a tremendous treasure in nature and will realize that it is holy and sacred. We will see God reaching out to us in every wind that blows, every sunrise and sunset, every cloud in the sky, every flower that blooms, and every leaf that fades.

OSWALD CHAMBERS

The longer I live, the more my mind dwells upon the beauty and the wonder of the world.

JOHN BURROUGHS

Look up at all the stars in the night sky and hear your Father saying, "I carefully set each one in its place. Know that I love you more than these." Sit by the lake's edge, listening to the water lapping the shore and hear your Father gently calling you to that place near His heart.

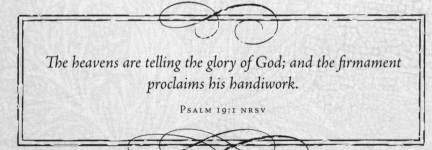

*The heavens are telling the glory of God; and the firmament proclaims his handiwork.*

PSALM 19:1 NRSV

TREASURE IN NATURE

God, our God! God the one and only! Love God, your God, with your whole heart: love him with all that's in you, love him with all you've got! Write these commandments that I've given you today on your hearts. Get them inside of you and then get them inside your children. Talk about them wherever you are, sitting at home or walking in the street; talk about them from the time you get up in the morning to when you fall into bed at night. Tie them on your hands and foreheads as a reminder; inscribe them on the doorposts of your homes.

DEUTERONOMY 6:4–9 MSG

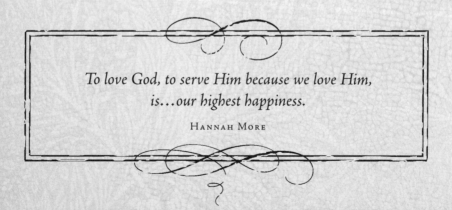

*To love God, to serve Him because we love Him,*
*is…our highest happiness.*

HANNAH MORE

## WITH ALL YOU'VE GOT

_____

_____

_____

_____

_____

_____

_____

_____

_____

_____

_____

_____

_____

_____

_____

_____

_____

_____

## THE SEA REMAINS THE SEA

Dear Lord, today I thought of the words of Vincent Van Gogh, "It is true that there is an ebb and flow, but the sea remains the sea." You are the sea. Although I may experience many ups and downs in my emotions and often feel great shifts in my inner life, you remain the same.... There are days of sadness and days of joy; there are feelings of guilt and feelings of gratitude; there are moments of failure and moments of success; but all of them are embraced by your unwavering love. My only real temptation is to doubt your love...to remove myself from the healing radiance of your love. To do these things is to move into the darkness of despair. O Lord, sea of love and goodness, let me not fear too much the storms and winds of my daily life, and let me know that there is ebb and flow... but that the sea remains the sea. Amen.

HENRI J. M. NOUWEN

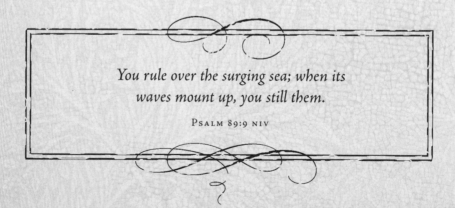

*You rule over the surging sea; when its waves mount up, you still them.*

PSALM 89:9 NIV

# THE SEA REMAINS THE SEA

## Giving and Receiving

If you give, you will receive. Your gift will return to you in full measure, pressed down, shaken together to make room for more, and running over. Whatever measure you use in giving—large or small—it will be used to measure what is given back to you.

LUKE 6:38 NLT

Give generously, for your gifts will return to you later.

ECCLESIASTES 11:1 NLT

The world of the generous gets larger and larger.... The one who blesses others is abundantly blessed; those who help others are helped.

PROVERBS 11:24–25 MSG

It is more blessed to give than to receive.

ACTS 20:35 KJV

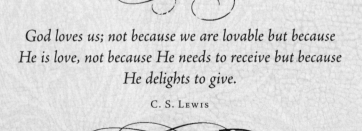

*God loves us; not because we are lovable but because He is love, not because He needs to receive but because He delights to give.*

C. S. LEWIS

## GIVING AND RECEIVING

_____

_____

_____

_____

_____

_____

_____

_____

_____

_____

_____

_____

_____

_____

_____

_____

_____

_____

_____

_____

_____

## His Beautiful World

The God who holds the whole world in His hands wraps himself in the splendor of the sun's light and walks among the clouds.

Forbid that I should walk through Thy beautiful world with unseeing eyes: Forbid that the lure of the market-place should ever entirely steal my heart away from the love of the open acres and the green trees: Forbid that under the low roof of workshop or office or study I should ever forget Thy great overarching sky.

JOHN BAILLIE

Our Creator would never have made such lovely days, and given us the deep hearts to enjoy them, above and beyond all thought, unless we were meant to be immortal.

NATHANIEL HAWTHORNE

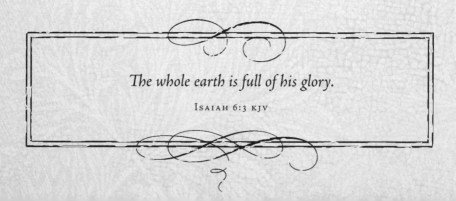

*The whole earth is full of his glory.*

ISAIAH 6:3 KJV

HIS BEAUTIFUL WORLD

_____

_____

_____

_____

_____

_____

_____

_____

_____

_____

_____

_____

_____

_____

_____

_____

_____

_____

_____

_____

Praise ye the Lord. Praise God in his sanctuary: praise him in the firmament of his power. Praise him for his mighty acts: praise him according to his excellent greatness. Praise him with the sound of the trumpet: praise him with the psaltery and harp. Praise him with the timbrel and dance: praise him with stringed instruments and organs. Praise him upon the loud cymbals: praise him upon the high sounding cymbals. Let every thing that hath breath praise the Lord. Praise ye the Lord.

PSALM 150:1–6 KJV

*May your life become one of glad and unending praise to the Lord as you journey through this world.*

TERESA OF AVILA

## PRAISE AND WORSHIP

_____

_____

_____

_____

_____

_____

_____

_____

_____

_____

_____

_____

_____

_____

_____

_____

_____

_____

_____

## GIFTS OF LOVE

Gratitude consists in a watchful, minute attention to the particulars of our state, and to the multitude of God's gifts, taken one by one. It fills us with a consciousness that God loves and cares for us, even to the least event and smallest need of life.

HENRY EDWARD MANNING

To be grateful is to recognize the Love of God in everything He has given us—and He has given us everything. Every breath we draw is a gift of His love, every moment of existence is a gift of grace.

THOMAS MERTON

The impetus of God's love comes from within Himself, to share with us His life and love. It is a beautiful, eternal gift, held out to us in the hands of love. All we have to do is say "Yes!"

JOHN POWELL, S.J.

*Let them give thanks to the Lord for his unfailing love.*

PSALM 107:8-9 NIV

GIFTS OF LOVE

_____

_____

_____

_____

_____

_____

_____

_____

_____

_____

_____

_____

_____

_____

_____

_____

_____

_____

## I WILL CARRY YOU

Listen to me…you whom I have upheld since you were conceived, and have carried since your birth. Even to your old age and gray hairs I am he, I am he who will sustain you. I have made you and I will carry you; I will sustain you and I will rescue you.

ISAIAH 46:3–4 NIV

He shall feed his flock like a shepherd: he shall gather the lambs with his arm, and carry them in his bosom, and shall gently lead those that are with young.

ISAIAH 40:11 KJV

*They travel lightly whom God's grace carries.*

THOMAS À KEMPIS

# I WILL CARRY YOU

_____

_____

_____

_____

_____

_____

_____

_____

_____

_____

_____

_____

_____

_____

_____

_____

_____

_____

## THE RHYTHM OF LOVE

Let God have you, and let God love you—and don't be surprised if your heart begins to hear music you've never heard and your feet learn to dance as never before.

MAX LUCADO

God knows the rhythm of my spirit and knows my heart thoughts. He is as close as breathing.

From the heart of God comes the strongest rhythm—the rhythm of love. Without His love reverberating in us, whatever we do will come across like a noisy gong or a clanging symbol. And so the work of the human heart, it seems to me, is to listen for that music and pick up on its rhythms.

KEN GIRE

*Then those who sing as well as those who play the flutes shall say, "All my springs of joy are in you."*

PSALM 87:7 NASB

_____

_____

_____

_____

_____

_____

_____

_____

_____

_____

_____

_____

_____

_____

_____

## FEAR NOT

Don't be afraid, I've redeemed you. I've called your name. You're mine. When you're in over your head, I'll be there with you. When you're in rough waters, you will not go down. When you're between a rock and a hard place, it won't be a dead end—Because I am God, your personal God, The Holy of Israel, your Savior. I paid a huge price for you…! *That's* how much you mean to me! *That's* how much I love you!

ISAIAH 43:1–4 MSG

If God be for us, who can be against us?

ROMANS 8:31 KJV

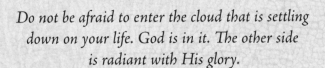

*Do not be afraid to enter the cloud that is settling down on your life. God is in it. The other side is radiant with His glory.*

L. B. COWMAN

FEAR NOT

_____

_____

_____

_____

_____

_____

_____

_____

_____

_____

_____

_____

_____

_____

_____

_____

_____

_____

## LOVE ONE ANOTHER

You who have received so much love share it with others. Love others the way that God has loved you, with tenderness.

MOTHER TERESA

Let Jesus be in your heart,

Eternity in your spirit,

The world under your feet,

The will of God in your actions.

And let the love of God shine forth from you.

CATHERINE OF GENOA

Every single act of love bears the imprint of God.

*Dear friends, since God so loved us, we also ought to love one another.... If we love one another, God lives in us and his love is made complete in us.*

1 JOHN 4:11–12 NIV

LOVE ONE ANOTHER

_____

_____

_____

_____

_____

_____

_____

_____

_____

_____

_____

_____

_____

_____

_____

_____

## SOURCE OF WONDER

I would maintain that thanks are the highest form of thought, and that gratitude is happiness doubled by wonder.

G. K. CHESTERTON

Dear Lord, grant me the grace of wonder. Surprise me, amaze me, awe me in every crevice of your universe.... Each day enrapture me with your marvelous things without number. I do not ask to see the reason for it all; I ask only to share the wonder of it all.

JOSHUA ABRAHAM HESCHEL

> May our lives be illumined
> by the steady radiance
> renewed daily,
> of a wonder,
> the source of which
> is beyond reason.
>
> DAG HAMMARSKJÖLD

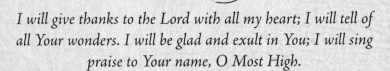

*I will give thanks to the Lord with all my heart; I will tell of all Your wonders. I will be glad and exult in You; I will sing praise to Your name, O Most High.*

PSALM 9:1–2 NASB

SOURCE OF WONDER

_____

_____

_____

_____

_____

_____

_____

_____

_____

_____

_____

_____

_____

_____

_____

_____

_____

_____

Whatsoever things are true, whatsoever things are honest, whatsoever things are just, whatsoever things are pure, whatsoever things are lovely, whatsoever things are of good report; if there be any virtue, and if there be any praise, think on these things.

PHILIPPIANS 4:8 KJV

The fountain of beauty is the heart, and every generous thought illustrates the walls of your chamber.

FRANCIS QUARLES

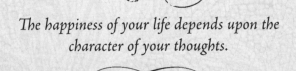

*The happiness of your life depends upon the character of your thoughts.*

THINK ON THESE THINGS

_____

_____

_____

_____

_____

_____

_____

_____

_____

_____

_____

_____

_____

_____

_____

_____

_____

## UNFAILING LOVE

God is not only the answer to a thousand needs, He is the answer to a thousand wants. He is the fulfillment of our chief desire in all of life. For whether or not we've ever recognized it, what we desire is unfailing love. Oh, God, awake our souls to see—You are what we want, not just what we need. Yes, our life's protection, but also our heart's affection. Yes, our soul's salvation, but also our heart's exhilaration. Unfailing love. A love that will not let me go!

BETH MOORE

The greatest honor we can give God is to live gladly because of the knowledge of His love.

JULIAN OF NORWICH

*Satisfy us in the morning with your unfailing love, that we may sing for joy and be glad all our days.*

PSALM 90:14 NIV

# UNFAILING LOVE

_____

_____

_____

_____

_____

_____

_____

_____

_____

_____

_____

_____

_____

_____

_____

_____

_____

_____

_____

> *We need time to dream, time to remember,*
> *and time to reach the infinite. Time to be.*
>
> GLADYS TABER

_____

_____

_____

_____

_____

_____

_____

_____

_____

_____

_____

_____

_____

_____